to Dr. Kerry Hasler-Brooks, without whom these words would lie unwritten,
to Marilyn Nelson and Panic! at the Disco for their inspirational way with words,
&
to Justin, without whom I would not believe in happy endings

intricacies are just cracks in the wall

by Sarah Margaret Henry

part i: gradual crucifixion

i am

Cassidy.
Cass-i-dy, *say it loud, say it proud,*
My momma always told me.
All three syllables, not crushed
Between your teeth like
Ice
You tried too fast to drink.

A mumble meant to take up
As little space as humanly possible.

Unabashedly take up space my momma said,
And paint it as many colors as you can find,
Because baby, you deserve all the sunrises
The world has to offer.

Cassie?
"It's Cassidy," I smile and imagine
My mother planting a kiss on my forehead
With a *go get 'em, baby*
As I walk straight into the office
To interview for a future
That is mine for the taking.

canvas

I step softly
Into an apartment that,
On paper,
I know is mine.
Its walls white
And rooms
Cavernous,
Begging to be filled
And I wonder if there is enough
Of me to fill this aching need.

Three days.

Step 1: Tomorrow,
The movers come, with boxes that hold
My life inside them.

Step 2: The next,
I will untangle the webs,
Separating the trinkets from the
Plastic plates and decorative pillows
My mom insisted I own.

Step 3: The day after,
I will straighten the photographs,
Wading through
The unpacked boxes and catching
My toes on ones that beg to be unwrapped.

Step 4: The following Monday,
I start my first day as an editorial assistant
And the next chapter begs to be written.

absence

The next day is a barrage of boxes,
So much so that I lose count
Before they all reach the truck
And I never knew my life was this vast. Or perhaps cluttered.
My mother waves goodbye as I
Stow myself in my minimom van
And I think I catch a tear in the rearview mirror.

But perhaps it's wishful thinking.

She is skipping my move-in day for a yoga class after all.

distill

We find parking near enough
And the movers begin to unload my life as I fumble the keys
Into the door I have only opened once before.
They follow me in and we
Begin this dance of carrying
Box after box, passing each other
And wondering how often we have to smile
Or nod after each passing.
After half the boxes make their way into piles
Onto what will be a living room floor,
I start to sort the haphazard cacophony that has become
These masses of objects.
Nietzsche?
I turn to find one of the movers peering over my shoulder
And his eyes brighten with a smile at my surprise.
"Oh, yes," I reply, because I know he intended a question
But not the answer he searched for.
I've always been more of a Kant man myself he offers,
His eyes glazing over at the sea of the books below us.
I reach down and offer him my laboriously annotated copy of *The Critique
        of Judgement.*
"As have I. But I find that in the dismal wretchedness of the world, it's
        always comforting to partake in the company of someone even
        more cynical than I."
He counters with *Well wouldn't you rather have tea with a creator?*
"Kant didn't create, he merely categorized artists that did."
Touche. He grinned.
Well, back to work. You keep sorting, Socrates.

the first one-sided conversation

Flipping through books,
Prolonging the decision to organize
By author or subject
On the Ikea bookshelf, I now realize,
Lies unbuilt, still boxed one room over.

From Kant falls an annotated business card.

> Hey Socrates,
> Since you're so interested in commiserating, Tuesday, 7:00, Pints Bar & Grille?
>> -Jack

balancing civility

Work is a castle
I must maintain, guard my garden
From aphids there,
Guard my eaves from the
Drop drip of the pitter patter of gossiped rain here,
Mend the alliance between
The kingdoms of sales and marketing,
Even if it means giving Susan's hand,
The forty finest oxen, and paperclips
To Robert in matrimony.

Home, on the other hand,
Is a lighthouse.

rooted

A booth at T.J Rockwell's
Seems all too cozy
When just an hour before
We were divided by department,
Sequestered in hedges of desks
Beyond a neatly lined patio of office spaces.
Zara likes her whiskey neat
And Sam's stories always meander
Beyond their intended punchline
And Trayvon isn't ashamed
To drink some concoction that calls
For a cherry on the side.
They're all too loud
And tell me all too much
But I'm warm inside when I drive home,
Opening my windows to
The early August Harrisburg air
And think I'm starting
To like it here.

all i have is enough

Pretty Odd mumbles on the record player
My grandfather almost pitched
When he declared
No one listens with this rubbish anymore.

I saved it from the curbside.

He was fascinated with the
Intricacies of what could fit
On a compact disc, how much could he hold
In so little space.
It just makes ergonomic sense, Cassie.

I learned to stop correcting him
When my mom said he doesn't remember much
Past his late fifties.

I, on the other hand,
Love the clunky monstrosity
That plays music that came out
Decades after it grew obsolete,
The Victrola my megaphone for almost
Anything in vogue on Amazon.com.

The harmonies seep into the painted walls
As my organization decisions grow
Less and less sure as the
Bottle of White Zinfandel grows
Less and less full
And I conduct
Panic's old crew
As they reinvent love.

Who could ask for any more?
Who could have more?

hurry up and wait

Waist belted,
Hair tucked,
Legs shaved.

I make my way to Pint's,
Not the place I'd pick,
But it might be a favorite of his,
So I vow to try something new
And let this city sing to me.

I'm half way through a Chardonnay,
Half ready to call it a bust,
Half ready to admit I've been stood up,
Ready to turn and leave
When he arrives, dressed to the nines
And orders me something *less pink*.

latency

Saturday mornings are mine.
I'm up early enough to add
Generally unused hours to the day,
My coffee percolating and
My mouth puckering as I force myself
To eat a half grapefruit
(One spoonful of sugar, spread for taste)
Because citrus always
Jolts
My mind awake
From its previously underwhelming state.

I never let myself shower until
I've got something down—
A poem, anecdote, witty joke—
Something, so long as I can say
"I wrote something today."

You made your way onto the pages this morning.

i am a curiousity

Midtown Scholar, both bookstore and coffeeshop,
Our talk circles the small, overcrowded
Room boasting clanking cups and
Businessmen arguing and high school
Heartthrobs crooning too close to be polite
In the corner. I can barely hear him
Over the din but the way he shapes
Words with his thin mouth makes me smile
Nonetheless. He explains
His job, something with numbers and
Data sheets, how he was only filling in
For his buddy who was too hung over to
Help move me. *It's like the universe*
Wanted us to meet, he says sarcastically
As he assures me in the next breath
That he doesn't ascribe to destiny.
I nodded too long after some comment
About the weather and he smirks as he says
You can't really hear me, can you?
I nod once more.
He grabs a book from the shelves lining the shop,
Peers over his shoulder, puts a delicate finger to his lips,
And tears lose the copyright page.
He returns the book to its place and stares deeply
Into me, his gaze, piercing and sure.
He scribbles, delicately, along the margins,
And I try to read upside down,
But he catches me and covers his work with his elbow.
He glances up once more and
Writes one last line.

He hands me the first poem
He ever wrote to me.

week long tennis match — 40 - love

It always takes you
Hours
To text me.

Sometimes days.

I wonder whether it's worth
Responding,
Tell myself
"Last text" then he can make a move.
"Ball's in your court, buddy,"
I say, my voice more smug than sure.

My place. Tonight. You said The Princess Bride was your favorite movie?

i don't know how to tell you

Your couch sits four comfortably
But we fit nicely
With you laying behind me.

An hour before, when I started to fall
Asleep on your shoulder,
You suggested we lay down to rest.
Your body heat, cheek on my neck,
Is perfect.

 But I do not love
The way your trailing fingers
Lift and wander under my shirt.

I think
Surely he'll stop eventually.

my waist is a focal point

You really do look
Stunning in that dress, Cassie.
Before I can say
It's Cassi-
Just the way it pulls in your figure.
I could put my pinky around your waist.
The sun does wonders for your smile
And I close my eyes, laying back
On the blanket we brought to Riverside Park.

Since you're acting so sweet,
I'll choose the path of least resistance
And let the pet name slide.

I'm not afraid
But not entirely wanting, either,
But he barely gives me enough breath
To collect a no from my lungs
But his hands are light like
Gossamer infinities
With an agenda
But I suppose this
Is a prerequisite for date five
So I suppose my clothes belong
On the floor
But his silence, lack of questions,
Lack of laughter, as though this is
A grave matter, a means to an end,
But before I can decide
He comes to a conclusion inside me
And leaves to throw away the reminder
In the bathroom trashcan.

But maybe I'm overthinking this.
Maybe love is meant to be more thoughtless than this.

reflections imposed on a mirror

I wonder how many minutes it will take before I
Hate
This dress on my body.
Too snug here, too baggy there
And this magenta leaves much
To be desired in relation to
Your complexion.
I should know, dear,
The mirror croons, taking a drag
Off her cigarette, her figure as thin as paper
And I wonder
If she regrets how she is forced to
Look like me
Every time I look at her.

nestle

His landlord's building was
Foreclosed, poor thing,
And now he's left without
A place to call his own
So, almost of their own accord,
His boxes begin stacking themselves in my kitchen.

This is perfect, you say, your arm around me.
I wanted us to move in together anyway.

deafening

He requires
Silence
Not quiet
To think
So I tiptoe across
Ikea carpets I
Paid for because
He
Just needs to think
And maybe if he
Thinks
For a goddamn minute
With
All I ask for is some peace and silence, is that too fucking much
The absence I give
Could you possibly stomp any louder?
Then maybe
Do you really need to breathe like that?
He will remember
God fucking damnit
That I am more than
Jesus Christ
A void.

all i can think about

It's a blister rubbing
Just below the skin,
Ready to burst,
But it's just beyond
My reach.

when absence is a welcome bedfellow

Maybe I just need to lie down,
Close my eyes, phone, door,
Find a pillow case soft enough
To suffocate the coos and moans
Of a world who wants all too much
Of me.

I'm trying to decide what made it a bad day.

Simple, quiet workflow,
Bland, predictable commute
Nothing to write home about
Coffeeshop, and I hear the door
To our apartment creak and I
Don't even notice my fingers clawing
And clutching our pillow case, willing
The bedroom door *stay shut.*

home is indefinite

How long has it been
Since I realized that a
Coffee shop feels more like home
Than the place I pay rent?

The titters of teacups on saucers
Making their way to wash bins,
Patrons weaving their way between
Mismatched tables and chairs
In no distinguishable floor pattern,
Women writing dissertations,
Men reading novels they think
Have impressive covers of
Sufficient academia, suitable
As a conversation starter that will end
With the subtle revelation of their —*je ne sais quoi*—
Intelligence?

A pair of men try to cajole their
Daughter to keep her popsicle in her
Mouth, rather than using it as a paintbrush, drawing circles
In lackadaisical, melting colors
On the white carpet.

I wonder what it is like to raise an artist.

Only the ticking clock on the wall
Behind me can tell
How much time has passed.

And only Jack, waiting, the marks of his pacing
Imprinted on the unvacuumed carpet,
Fuming in front of me can tell me
How much time I've wasted.
He asks where I was, barely
Pausing for an answer,
Before demanding another

To *why didn't you answer my calls?*
I tell him I left my phone at home
And he removes it from his pocket
And places it in my hand.

Don't.
Leave it.
Again.

Alone in the locked bathroom,
I look at the messages, the calls,
The livid voicemails and I can
Scarcely imagine
How you thought *I*
Was wasting time
When you spent your afternoon
Yelling into an inbox
That was 10 feet from you.

At least
He cares about me.

It's meant as a response
But instead,
It lilts as a question.

my (?) living room has its own atmosphere

My plants keep dying.
I stock our windowsill
With succulents, basil,
Cilantro, cat grass,
Unnamed greenery that
Allegedly
Is unkillable.
All they need is
Water and sunlight and
I offer them both and
All I hold is
Brown, crinkled leaves
That shatter themselves
Under my mourning touch.

Why does nothing
Seem to grow here?

festered

I've learned to ignore
The incessant quivers of my purse
As it vibrates angrily against the booth.
I'm trying to focus on Zara's
Weaving and winding tale that
I think
Is about her divorced parents
Deciding on who should keep the car
But as soon as the humming stops,
The silence is all the more mortifying,
Like running your tongue over
The hole where an abscessed tooth
Used to be.
I nod in all the right places,
But she can tell I'm off center
Even before I suddenly excuse myself
To freshen up.

Voicemail (23)

I steel myself against the bathroom sink,
Splash water on my cheeks
And turn the phone to silent.
I shoulder my purse
And try to stride into the restaurant
With the aura that
I only needed to touch up my mascara.

You're sitting on my side of the booth.

Cassie, I've been so worried about you.
"I told you yesterday that I –"
Let me walk you home.
I gesture to the pad thai that just arrived,
Starting to explain that –
It was lovely seeing you, Zara
He says in his iridescent smile,

Usually reserved for boardroom transactions,
As though he just
Landed the compromise
Months in the making
And I absentmindedly take his arm when offered,
Leaving Zara with the check and two untouched entrees.

I pay her the difference tomorrow morning.
She told me not to worry about it.
She found somewhere else to sit for lunch today.

catharsis is on sale for $16.99

No matter which way
I drive myself home from work
I always seem to end up
At Target.

I stroke each of the decorative pillows,
Wishing they were softer.
I wander through the faux plant aisle
And think of my dying azaleas
That were never meant for a window box.
I admire the seventeen different types of cutlery
And wonder what it would be like
To own a blender that didn't smoke
When you used too many frozen bananas
In a smoothie.

I don't want to say
I'm procrastinating,
Finding an oasis
Deep within the confines of Consumeristic Americana.
I can't decide
Why my apartment
Just doesn't seem like
Home
To me.

Perhaps, if I had one more tea towel
Or our windows had lighter curtains
Or we had just one more
Boho chic patterned rug
I wouldn't feel
Out of place
In our apartment.
Perhaps I need a shelf,
Rather than a pull-out couch
To fall asleep on at night,

Unbreakable and on display.

presently absent

Less is more
I've been told about what percentage
Of my body my clothes should show
I've been told about how often
I should speak
I've been told about how frequently
I text you
But I always see less of you
After a night out with friends
You still won't let me meet
And less always seems to just mean more
Vacancy.

those dizzy moments between standing and falling

Your vitriol leaves a sick,
Yellow taste in my mouth,
The room lingering with
The rank of demons you unearthed,
Powerful enough to carry the weight
Of the words you knew would stick.

the moments i allow myself to be angry

It endlessly ticks me off
That you have a clock
With four consecutive *I*'s
Rather than the proper Roman *IV*.
I did not tell you this for
Three weeks and four days
Because I knew
You would find my comment
Nit picky and *abhorrently predictable.*

It emerged
At the end of an argument
That began something like
This *is the asparagus you picked?*
And followed us to the car
And all the way home,
A crescendo that started
With eyerolls and muted indignation
That plateaued with
At least I'm not a selfish prude who parades around like she's goddamn Socrates
And my cheeks smarted at your
Volume, your proximity, your venom.
I roll back my shriveled shoulders
And puff out my chest
Before my diaphragm caves and I
Deflate, slamming the bedroom door
Behind me.

Late that night, when you fall asleep,
Hoarse, on the couch after
Yelling for hours, epithets and profanities
Like daggers through our bedroom door
I take the clock from its shelf,
And take it back to our bedroom,
Place it next to a more accurate time piece.

When you ask me a few weeks later
Where the *goddamn clock is*
I shrug
But I know
What it sounded like
Shattering at the bottom of an anonymous trashcan
In some forgotten alleyway
On my walk to work.

a paradox on the edge of hypocrisy

We cut down trees
To build
Apartments for birds
We just un-homed.

Perhaps the apology
Is best left
Unmanifested.

what i would say if you asked what waiting for you felt like.
but you never do.

I'm starting to feel
The worry knotting itself
Deep within my stomach,
Growing like weeds, tendrils
Climbing my insides and
Sucking life without sun or water.

It's 1:03am and my texts are
Still
Unanswered. I didn't
Even see you come home from work today.
I think you kissed my cheek before
You left for your morning commute.

I'm starting to forget.

I hear someone fumbling against
The door as though
That someone forgot where and
What a keyhole was
And they needed to investigate

The whole door with their bodyweight.

Before I can reach
The peephole, you come
Crashing through the door,
Sending me, back against the wall.

You mumble something about
Calming down, **backing off,**
Before I can even speak.
I look at your clothes, expecting
Blood, some sign of a fight, a limp,
But I soon discover that the only
Destruction is the pungent smell
Of your mouth when you speak
Breathlessly in my direction.
"Where have you been?" I try
To ask calmly because I know
You think asking too many questions
Is *nagging* and *obtuse* and *clingy*
To the highest degree.

Out.

With that, you enter the bedroom,
Pass out in your reeking suit and tie.

I sleep alone on the couch.
I can't tell if it's the smell or you that makes me sick.

breeding ground

I do not know which sin to wallow in,
Which inadequacy to offer blindly on a
Platter silver enough to please you, what to
Offer as a sacrifice worthy enough for your
Bare, naked teeth, what meat is bloody
Enough to satiate your weighted grin.
I've met the monsters and gargoyles that lie nestled
In your stomach, know how they make you weak because
They beg for more to eat and I wish
This symbiosis wasn't enough for me because
I am begging myself to wake up and see
That I am not happy living just as a
Body built to feed the beast burrowed
Inside your sickly skin, his home,
The light I thought I saw
When I asked, for the countless time,
If you loved me.

my heart and head keep debating before they realize they are on the same side

I sit in stairwells when the apartment's thoughts are
Too loud,
Pregnant with the idea that
Nothing really matters
And maybe staying with you
Is my latest phase of self-desecration
Or is it little more than an apathetic suicide?

I'm just letting the house of cards
Topple around me, leaving paperthin
Traces across my paperthin skin
And I don't care that the cards
Slice as they fall and maybe laying
Here
Is an act of resistance or
Passive acceptance of apocalypse
And I wonder if being an artist
Is an art of remembering or believing
Or perhaps hoping that

Someday

Things could be different.

a knot you never knew i untied

Skin caked dry with foundation I cried clean
You, I, the door, black mascara streaks.

part ii: perforated internment

shopping list

-Riesling
-Lean Cuisine X 5
-box of bow tie pasta
-heart of celery
-carrots
-pre-made roasted chicken
-low sodium chicken broth
-Chocolate Peanut Butter Cup Explosion Ice Cream
-Puffs Plus Lotion
-~~pack of razor blades~~

i knew you by a different name

Some say that you need
To let the child feel the heat
Off the burning stove to learn the word
Danger.

Maybe I just learned all too late.

Maybe danger was never a stove.

authenticity: a cabaret

It's just about midnight here,
Ladies and gentlemen,
And the star of the show
Is cooped up in an overpriced apartment
With little to no leg room,
Half a glass away
From the bottom of a half-priced,
Overly-sweet rosé
And I can't help but think
Of all the parts I'm supposed
To fall in love with playing.
Aren't girls my age supposed to love
Cappuccinos and throwbacks and
Sex and rebounds and
Books of poetry no one likes
Where the title is worth the price of admission?

This is coming of age
This is believing
This is loneliness masquerading as independence
This is giving in
This is the edge of breaking.

abscess

I come home from work
And drop my bag
As my raised eyes see that
My apartment is
Empty.

I fumble to my phone
And halfway dial for help
Before I realize
This is not a robbery.
I do a mental inventory.

Everything missing is his.

My apartment looks like a mouth
Filled with missing teeth
And I know they were rotting cavities
But I remember
He still has a key
And I sit in the middle of the
Post-op living room
And in the sterile, cavernous wake
Of the missing things.

And I wonder when I'll have the time
To install a second lock.

pulling pieces of you from my head

My hair is unendingly,
Relentlessly
Too long
Whether it be the length
Of a forefinger or
The width of
Fingernail,
Anything
I can yank
And pull and pinch as I grit
My teeth and rip
At anything that will tear,
Grasping at something that
Will leave a mark when it's
Gone.

metamorphosis

Bleach
Stains the air and the
Dye circles the drain
My eyes find different hair,
I paint a different face,
Maybe
If I can look a little differently
Than I do in pictures that
Can't help but hold you
Then I can breathe easy
Because this new body
Can't remember you.

all i am is on life support

There are days I demand myself
Write.
"Right," I roll my eyes
With the final ounce of gall
I have left
Like that
Will amount to anything.
The voice inside me
With anything worth uttering
Does not have the energy
To retaliate, her quiver
For striking back lies
Bereft of arrows.

Apathy
Will be the death of me
Because, like cancer,
It grows until your heart
Is all too heavy to function.

lovely, dark, and deep

I never knew rain could be so
Black, slick, sticking leaves
To the pavement to make for
One hell of a drive, the night
Is a passenger in my car,
Asking me to turn up
Metallica, not caring much for my
Unapologetic Joni Mitchell,
He envelops the car seat
And the road ahead, I drive
Deep into his belly,
Unsure if I'm already dead
Because all I see
Are headlights haloing my sight
And I'm unsure if I'm anointed
Or marked like the plague,
Because truth be told
I don't remember where the
Fuck I'm going
And the night resumes his seat, passenger side,
And suggests a breakdown
On a pair of train tracks
Or a head-on with an unsuspecting oak
And I don't know how to tell him
No
When I can't remember that
All I needed
Was milk from the supermarket.

life is not only flesh

I don't know that all life deserves
A body. I certainly don't believe
That I am worthy of flesh, my spirit
One meant more for whispered,
Windswept sentiments in the back forties
Of Ohio, the instantiation of a casual smile
Passed on a subway, the strength one admires
Of an oak tree. I do not think that
My existence is futile, I merely believe
That my corporeality would best be suited
For someone else, a soul breathed from the
Lungs who could not fathom death just yet.
The essence of my Platonic form could serve
The world much more eloquently in the
Elation one feels in the twinkle of a sunbeam.

I would be better breath than bone.

mostly blank pages

My poetry is growing smaller.

Clipped sentences, frugal words.

It's all I can manage to pen
Before
I sink
Back between the covers,
Dreading the sunlight that unendingly
Plagues my bedroom.

Too bright to sleep,
To taxing to wake.

what is left

I am a cup
Tipped to the side
And all that touches the table
Is a measly drop
Of water,
Insubstantial, insignificant,
And not nearly enough
To water anything worth growing.

claustrophobia is its own kind of cure

I don't
Want to write sonnets of his
Vacant stare or epics of the
Inside of closet sized spaces I grew
To know because only in a
Space so small could I feel
Safe from the alleyway that you used
As your bildungsroman, my lips,
Breast, thighs, unwilling actors.

i forget the sky

The act of
Being
Is a fragile one.
It takes the strength of
Infinities just to breathe,
It seems the more you learn,
The more your heart weighs
And you wonder if it's worth learning at all.
It's harder to stand
And when it's easier to fall,
You wonder if you should rise
If only to return
To the place you vowed
You'd never go again.
You wonder if you'll ever
Leave. You forget
What the sun looks like
When it isn't drowning in moonlight because
Where you went is a dark reflection of a memory
And joy doesn't translate through mirrors because
You cannot feel faded light.

I've never noticed how many knives act like they belong in my kitchen.

- *is it possible to think too much?*

I am not a construction site
With yellow tape that neatly states
Stay Out. Rather, I am
Rubble some man from
The back of the bar chose to explore,
Leafing through the pebbles and refuse,
Lightly fingering each rock,
Wondering *What could this*
Have once been? rather than
Asking the remains outright
How she felt that he dared
To touch her.

– i am not a curiosity

cheap replays and insatiable critics

I find it nearly
Impossible
To fall asleep at night,
The tendrils of the day
Weeping into my hair
Alternative realities of how I could have
Better lived life that day.
They snake around my eyes, slithering
Deep inside my ears, pulling and
Playing with my memories of my
Performance on day eight thousand four hundred seventy two of playing
The part of a neurotypical nobody,
Banal enough not to be noticed,
But personable enough not to be
Forgotten.

Every night, the critics roll in their reviews

Dropped the ball in Act I Scene II

Not sure what the plot is anyway

Stilted, sloppy dialogue. Did she really say
"You too" to the waiter who said
"Enjoy your food"?

And they all amount essentially to
Nothing more
Than a general insistence that I should
Permanently
Cancel this production

And I can't agree more.

rewiring

I wonder why I bother wasting time writing.
Words wet the page and
They dry, stay dormant,
Stagnantly sleeping,
Undisturbed beyond their
Act of creation.

With no one to read them,
Why write them at all?

And then I wondered when I started defining myself
By those around me, as though
They were barometers calibrated to measure
My worth.

how to end a blue period

I'm searching for the cure to end all ills.

Music seems an auspicious choice,
But one wrong track on a heartbreak mixtape
And you've got yourself a basket-case
Instead of a break-up victory speech.

Poetry, the same fatal flaw,
One misplaced word and you've
Written your own end
Rather than the way into her heart.

Laughter is allegedly the best medicine
But it fades and all you have
Is a sour broken rib,
Pained with the state of its own cure.

Art is much the same;
Show someone Picasso's blue period
And you've made a mirror rather than
Someone who dreams of something more.

distraction is its own kind of medicine

Books smell like
New beginnings, something borrowed,
Something new, a book whose cover
Is robin's egg blue.
It's the only kind of store I know that holds
Universes, pocket-sized multitudes
And I always spend more than I pictured
But what a bargain to buy a world for
$9.99 (plus tax, of course).

the last words i'll ever waste on you

At the noises pouring from your naked smile
That sound like they were supposed to be
Apologies
As though
Honey
Could set broken bones
As though
Sugar
Could stitch a gaping wound
As though
Your swollen, practiced tears
Could reach to touch
A heart your venom and knuckles calloused,
This heart, concrete set as sidewalk,
Years in the making,
An urban jungle of a path
Men trod along
Casually, intentionally, unforgivingly,
Because you taught me that I
Was a sideshow,
A stopping point between
Her and
Mrs. Right but
I am not your fucking princess
So leave your mulled and fermenting vocabulary
At the door you left
Ajar, open for
Scum and fleas masquerading
As modern gentlemen
Because I can't tell the difference,
You taught me that to be loved
I had to mask every bit of me
But I have watered
What you called weeds
That peeked between
The concrete you left
Over the garden I grew

And now my heart looks
Nothing like the littered alleyway
You once knew and
I stumbled, walking along
The path you grew
But I have walked miles on my own
And this garden doesn't look
Anything like you.

A Panicked! Crown of Sonnets

I.

We move along with some new passion, know
That days by days go by and I pick up
Guitar and you stamp collect, I suppose –
Whatever you filled me with, try your luck
But I know you can't drink nearly enough
To fill the void of what I meant to you.
No, not I, not my being, but a rough
Approximation for disposal, too
Easy to roll between your fingers, teeth,
Something that clinked against the chill, cool tile
When dropped, something that moaned on command, leave
That record player on repeat awhile,
Enough to give meaning to existence.
Oh, this is the beat of my heart, this is.

II.

Oh, this is the beat of my heart, this is
Breathing, this is touching carpet, my face,
This, reminding myself of existence
Beyond ravens that peck and then embrace,
Men that ransack with the excuse of love
And wonder if this, my apartment, is
A village, or is it just small enough
To be pillaged, but beyond all language,
Categorization only delays
The idea of you coming here, taking
Anything from a book to my body
Ripping pieces from the inside, breaking
Them against the weight of your manhood, now
But I regain repose and wonder how.

III.

But I regain repose and wonder how
Something simple as a broken tea cup
Could cut so deep and fully overcrowd
My mind, recalibrate the day, end up
Blinking, hear the chinking ceramic on
Tile, epithets, my goddamn body,
Limbs that never learned to move with honor
And grace my grandfather complained loudly
I lacked and instructed I pursue. In
The smashing, severing handle from cup
I see your knifelike eyes search, incessant,
Desperate to pull apart a vein to suck,
Pool blood thick enough to bathe in, red, dark
Cause these words are knives that often leave scars.

IV.

Cause these words are knives that often leave scars
And I can't quite tear your "worthless," "ugly,"
"Fat" verbiage from my "average" brain, with far
Too many rogue voices in my head, why
Not add one with a PhD? I do
What I swore I would never do and ask
For "Help, please." She had quite a few things to
Say about you. But she chose to speak last,
Listen first. We've only had a session
Or two, but I'm sleeping okay with stored
Seroquel like a lazy river in
My brain. I don't wake up scared anymore.
Sunsets pass, unpreoccupied with him,
And I would wait and watch the hours fall in.

V.

And I would wait and watch the hours fall in
Waiting for a sign to fall from the sky
Saying this isn't one big joke, a sin
God elaborately planned, tell me why
These visions of haunted men and twisted
Trees and dying cats and rotting flesh vines
Are just a joke that only someone with
Grand omnipotence could find the punch line.
What's the humor in watching me wake in
A cold sweat, sheets plastered to my chest, is
The light from the moon on my wall simply
Moonbeams or are they spiders lying in
Wait to crawl on my face? I shudder in
Dreams I inflate, painted skies in my brain.

VI.

Dreams I inflate, painted skies in my brain
I tell my psych, looking for answers and
She reveals that perhaps God had mainly
No part in the fatalistic nightmares.
It was merely a bad reaction to
A med not meant for me. A change of pace.
Wellbutrin SR. I'm calmer, feel new,
But it takes months to settle, find some space
And I realize that maybe this calm is
A lack of feeling anything at all.
We talk for a while, weigh the pros, cons, this
Feeling too little or too much: resolve?
We both agree, although it makes me sick,
Blue is better than being over it.

VII.

Blue is better than being over it.
I know now that feeling, touching this sense
Of existence, prodding at the rancid
Sore lets me know that not just emptiness
Is nestled deep within my core. While this
Pain does not make me Cassidy, I might
As well wring a silver lining from these
Litanies of rotting clouds, set my sight
On something beyond wallowing, drink of
Their emptiness and move along. They bleed,
Follow me, envelop me in rain, but
Sunshine generally finds its way in beams.
Clouds suffocate the night, fill my airway,
The clock just makes the colors turn to gray.

VIII.

The clock just makes the colors turn to gray
And I wonder if wandering outside
This apartment that seems to grow away
From the sun as the winter bleeds spring is
Worth a try. At least for a while. I take
A walk along Riverside Park, see dogs
Traipsing with their walkers who try to make
Them take steps akin to a steady jog
To no avail. Bridges stand, resolute,
Commemorating some politician
I don't care to think about, waning truth.
And I sit on a bench meant for more than one
And I embrace the lonely and I see
Thoughts of past lovers. They'll always haunt me.

IX.

Thoughts of past lovers, they'll always haunt me,
Waiting in the shadows of untidy
Closets to wrap scarves, inadequacies,
Around my neck, pull me tight, I can't breathe,
They whisper threats, lies, knives so frequently
I now have them memorized by rote and
You stare at me from the fridge I can't clean
Of your condiments I can't bear, can't stand,
To touch, as though taking this ketchup from
Its shelf will unleash the memories of
Your wrath and disease, your false martyrdom
Haunting every room, closet, doorway, hall
This apartment, every piece of sweet, poor
Me. There is nothing else there at my door.

X.

Me. There is nothing else there at my door,
Just me, only Cas, nothing more, solely
A shadow slowly growing some color,
Metastasizing into a body,
More than a wakeless spirit, someone who
Takes up space, someone who dances between
Cluttered living room coffee tables, to
Move, simply because she can. Full, serene,
I revel in the emptiness of the
Apartment. There is so much more space for
Me to grow, live, breathe, realize myself. These
Loose pieces of me found stuck between floor
And couch for far too long. I live instead,
This symphony buzzing in my head.

XI.

This symphony buzzing in my head
When I walk to work, when I take the bus
To the grocery store and sure, I'll admit
There are times when the music will grow rough,
Hit a snag on a minor key, but some
Coffee, me time, journaling, call to mom,
Text friends, perforated isolation
Helps to fix. We add Risperdal to the
Effexor mix and I sleep in vibrant
Color but I sleep through the night and I'll
Take what I can get. I am vigilant,
I am less in tears and more I smile,
More writing letters to myself, of course.
Whether near or far, I am always yours.

XII.

Whether near or far, I am always yours,
And I wish to whatever God will hear
That I wasn't. I feel this small piece pulse
In its absence, flesh pumping along its tear,
I run fingers along the grooves of its
Emptiness and know beyond doubt that you
Hold it far from me. I'm building up bits
Of a temple for me. I deserve to
Adorn my body with the finest jewels
Twenty dollars can buy and I will soak
Myself in lilac and Epsom salt pools
And won't wrap myself in the sheets I woke
Up in when I was with you. Still I know
You're behind my eyelids when I'm alone.

XIII.

You're behind my eyelids when I'm alone
And I try to keep my eyes wide open
As though that is the one answer, as though
I don't need sleep, as though I will and can
Avoid eye contact with the man who looks
Just like you in Broad Street Market but I
Realize that I am strong enough, it took
Too long, to decide that I won't waste time
Being afraid of you anymore. That
I fear not for me, but the next fearful
Girl who falls for you. I pray for her at
Night if I remember before I fall
Asleep. If she's okay, I want to know.
I'm the light blinking: the end of the road.

IXV.

I'm the light blinking, the end of the road
And refuse to waste pages putting eyes
On you, because when I write, I unload
Monsters, immortalize, legitimize
Those who don't have any more life than what
I speak into them, and I need to write
Them so I can pour the stagnant water
From my head before it breeds insects, light
The match to burn the bodies and I won't
Owe them any more life than this. Without
Words, they suffocate. Now I really don't
Care how you're gasping for breath, mine a mouth
That will feed you no longer. Fuck, just go.
We move along with some new passion, no?

XV.

We move along with some new passion, know
Oh, this is the beat of my heart, this is—
But I regain repose and wonder how,
'Cause these words are knives and often leave scars
And I would wait and watch the hours fall in
Dreams, I inflate, painted skies in my brain.
Blue is better than being over it;
The clock just makes the colors turn to grey.
Those thoughts of past lovers, they'll always haunt
Me. There is nothing else there at my door.
This symphony still buzzing in my head;
Whether near or far, I am always yours.
You're behind my eyelids when I'm alone.
I'm the light blinking; the end of the road.

my lightless tunnel has moonbeams

Bedroom ceiling, silenced alarm,
Pull the covers back, take meds
Before I forget, before I brew the
Daily coffee I so desperately need
To tell me it's time to be.
Take a few sips, contemplate
The tulips in the window box
Trying so desperately to grow.
Pull back the curtain, step inside
The shower, let it warm the bones
That mourned the shedding of fleece lined
Socks and an oversized sweater.
Lather what little hair I have,
Rub the bar over my cracking skin
And I stop.

I heard myself humming.

It's been too long since my shower
Made music of me.

my mother's house is a welcome stranger

My mother's house is one
Cloaked in trees, the evergreen
Offering unending protection while the
Sunshine soldiers of dogwood and maple
Shed themselves before first frost,
Changing with the season as my mother
Rearranges the furniture.

This rug is just so in, dear.
Oh, I can't believe you ever let me buy that couch.
I really wish I hadn't lost those curtains in the divorce.
He still doesn't know I took the china, though.

I sit, draped in clearance rack designer blankets that feel as soft as
Anything I could buy at Target,
And watch the sun bleed through the peak in her triangle window
That consumes the entire east wall of the great room.

This is the type of window I'd want to watch a hurricane through.

part iii. self-germination

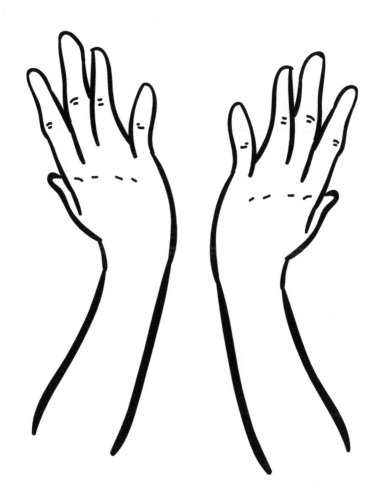

reflections in a pho3mein

I sit alone in
Pho3Mein and it's
More antiseptic than I imagined.

Perhaps
They didn't expect
Me, party of one,
An hour before closing on a
Tuesday.

The floors are wet with an
Unseen mop and the tiles
Dry beneath my impatient stomach.
By the doorway
Is an out-of-season Christmas tree
Whispering *I too*
Am an American.

The tinsel matches

The lights from the Coke Cooler,
But the faux rust colored stucco
Over the take out counter
And the paper
Folding divider, watercolored with bamboo,
Are in tension.

This tension sits comfortably
In my stomach because I do
Not belong to the pho and
Spring rolls that coax my tongue
Toward joy.

I ask for a bowl
To go
But I know
The magic will be lost
To a microwave
And the chatter of a table
Meant for more than me
Where slurping is impolite
And small talk is prerequisite.

reflections in zara's apartment

Wikipedia says
A lapdog is
A dog small enough to
– Comfortably–
Lie in a person's arms and *is*
Temperamentally predisposed to do so.
I turn my phone so all 87 pounds
Of Poncho can see that he
Is not,
In fact,
A lapdog. But the phone
Does no use because
He slides his muzzle
Between my fingertips, placing
Two yellow lab paws on
My chest and two on
My knees as if to say
Well maybe, if you quit your talking
And put that damn phone down,
There would be just enough room
For me.
I roll my eyes as he kneads my thighs
And curls up like a mountain lion sized cat
And as he drifts to dreams of
Heaven
That don't seem all too far from this,
I think
Well
"He certainly is temperamentally predisposed"
And that alone is more than enough
For me.

reflections on a coffee cup

Rain smells like
Healing. I sit,
My hand mugged with something
Sweet and caffeinated, and
Thunder rolls and clouds billow
Like an unfolded cotton snow.
Fat raindrops wrap wet and heavy
Against the window pane
And the uneven
Tap tap tap
Harkens to my mother's hands
Heavy against the steering wheel,
Fingers tapping to Aretha's latest hit
Even though Mama never could quite catch rhythm or beat.

The rain tastes like mornings
Mama made with dough,
Little biscuits, fluffed and
Buttered and melting in my mouth.

I wish it was all this simple:
Rain, myself, and coffee.
The trinity of an early Monday morning.

i am an ode unto myself

I want to write about Myself. I need
To fall in love with all my gaited steps.
The rapture caught in sunsetted hair lets
The muse believe she's breath of my body,

The aching of this insolvable "be"
Or not. He begs me answer, I forget
These pages are not mirrors, only dense
What ifs; no Denmark prince gives a shit about me.

I feather my arms with quotes, those likely
Dead things, plucked from forgotten upper clefts
Of tasteless palates, the ones language left.
Their words are beauty I can pay to keep.

The winged forearms I never noticed
Faintly undulate: desperate, now flightless.

weighted space

I don't remember
What it means
To share space
With others, bumping
Elbows, holding paper
Plates, filled with
Potluck pad Thai,
Baked ziti, curry
Chicken with sauce
That soaks through
Rice, the plate,
So you layer
Your lap with
Paper napkins, and
Carry on the
Conversation as though
Your jeans aren't
Destined for disaster.
They talk between
Sips of sweet
Wine, Blackberry Merlot:
Work, drama, films,

Who is seeing
Who. Zara, one
Hand clasping a
Glass and my
Wrist, pulls me
And my smorgasbord
Into the kitchen.
She mumbles, slurs
Something about *getting*
Back out there /
Perfect guy for
You / Shoot him
A text. She
Gives a one-armed
Embrace, plants a
Kiss on my
Cheek, and I
Am left in
The kitchen with
A number, a
Name, and a
Knot in my
Stomach.

initiating contact

Hey, Cas! It's Oliver. I guess Zara's trying to set us up, huh?

Of course, Cas. I would love that.

Cas. Cassidy. Can I call you Cassidy? You're okay. I understand. Probably too well. If you need space, that's fine, if you want to talk, I can listen. Just let me know what you need, okay?

Absolutely. Let me know if I can do anything for you, Cassidy.

Hey, it's Cas. We met at
Hey. Met you at
It was great to meet you!
You looked really nice yester
Hey, so I know this is crazy, but Zara gave me your number and
Is this Oliver? Zara gave me your number and
Hey. This is really scary for me. I just got out of a really abusive
relationship and I don't know if I'm ready yet.
Hey. It's Cas.

Yeah, I suppose so, haha.
Can I be honest with you?

Okay. Here is goes.
I just got out of an abusive relationship and I don't know
if I'm ready to "get back out there," you know?
Sorry, that was probably too much.

Thanks, Oliver.
You're too sweet.
I think I need some time.

A WEEK LATER
Hey. Weird question. Do you want to go bowling on Friday?

that space between something and nothing

Don't feel bad when I
Destroy *you, Cassidy*
He smiles confidently.
They didn't call me
Mr. Turkey in 5th grade for nothing.

"Consider me properly warned,"
I smile, picking out the pink ball
From the racks.
He compliments my neon choice,
And sets our names up in the system
As
The Destroyer
And
Ummm Cassidy
Because I hesitated when he asked
What I wanted as a nickname.
I stick out my tongue and
Turn my glare into a game face.

I lose, heroically so.

solitude is not a prison sentence

I'm falling in love with being
Lonely. The air up here is
Sweet, light, with space big enough
To grow, my apartment not
A cell but a window-box
And I am soaking in sunlight
I never remember feeling in my bedroom before
And I can sing as loudly and
As badly as I want, my yowls
Barreling their way up to
Heaven because I am
Praiseworthy and my life is something
To give thanks and shout amen for.

overthinking, lack of air

He's picking me up at
8:00, three minutes from now,
That's if you believe the stove,
7:57 on the kitchen clock,
7:58 on the microwave,
And I keep pressing
Home on my phone,
So frequently, waiting for a text
To say
I can't make it.
I never really liked you anyway.
That I'm afraid the button will break
And the knock on the door at
7:59 on the stove
(8:00 on the microwave)
Hardens my bones and I
Robotically answer the door
As I am programmed to do
And I start to mumble a
"Hello"
But it comes out only
As air and I think
I hear him saying
Cassidy, are you there?
Before I clutch the closest chair
And proceed to break,
Tears, shuddering, the whole
Nine yards of ineptability,
Quaking proof that I am
Not ready for this, I haven't
Worn this dress since he
Left and it feels tight
Around my neck and
Everything is black and
Then I feel a
Blanket. Draped around my
Shoulders. I touch

Upholstery, and I know
I'm sitting on a couch.
My couch.
I blink back vision
And you are sitting
Beside me
Not close enough
To touch. You ask
Are you okay?
And I say yes
And you ask
Could I hold your hand?
And I say yes
And we sit in silence.
I breathe.
We missed
Our 8:15 reservation.
I asked if you cared.
You said sitting with me
Was *a joy unto itself.*

dates don't come with instruction manuals

A week later
We remake reservations
And I wear a different dress
And he drives slowly
And we arrive
And look at the menu
In the window while
We wait the forty-five minute wait
For the reservations
We were on time for.
We stand outside
Because the lobby was
Filled with heavy air
And glances from people
Who seemed to know
My dress was from Gap
And despise me for it.
Everything on the menu is
In French and is

Swimming with oysters or
In beurre monté
As though I'm
Just supposed to know
What that is before entering.
Wikipedia does, Oliver says,
And it is
Butter.
They could have just said
Butter.
But then they couldn't charge $47 for it Oliver shrugs.
We cancel our reservations.
We wander down to Brothers Pizzeria
A few blocks up the street and he challenges me
To see who can fit more
Onion rings in their mouth at once
And we order a calzone and a pie
Because we just can't decide
And we have to roll ourselves
Out to the car, heavy with grease and cheese,
But I feel light, light as air.

fancy thinking the beast was something you could hunt and kill

— William Golding, Lord of the Flies

I'm reading *Lord of the Flies* for the first time
Because he was
Horrified and
Aghast
That I have not yet read it.
I finish it in an afternoon,
Sip my cup of coffee,
Think of poor old Piggy
And the folly of budding manhood,
And wonder why
He loves it so much.
I shoot him a text to ask.

Because he answers as though it was obvious
It reminds us what a godforsaken
Mess the world would be
Without women to run it.

love isn't always a choice

I waited
Two months
To ask you what you meant
When you said
I understand. Probably too well
When I said
I once loved a man
Who loved me in digestible pieces
That he could take and eat
As he pleased.

You squeezed my hand,
Looked down at the ground,
As though
The answer was written in tile.

Sometimes, you breathed,
Fathers aren't all they're cracked up to be.

I squeezed your hand back,
A language louder than
What my words could mean.

I told you to take your time.
You can tell me,

Someday,

When you're ready.

swaying to a city's symphony

You and I live somewhere between now and a finger painted night
Our colors soft and waiting, touch me please, breathe the rain,
Flight on benches built for home-starved frames, drink the light
Under fingertips built for catching, cars crossing a pedestrian lane
Weathered and kissed by time, you, I, hips tease a beat
To words mouths alone cannot possibly explain.
Your tactile tongue, my light, my eyes, my cheek, a novella on my feet,
Waiting for taxis that will never come, an owl cry
Dresses my ears with something bright, lonely naked street,
Your wrists held deftly under my forefinger, thumb, pulse laden goodbye,
Skin echoed in city night lights and skylines, temptless poets never reach
    that height
Of you, I, window panes, stained glass, fractured veins painting an
    amaretto sky.

a linguist's vulnerability

I am a writer who is
A small dragon,
Spritely spitfire,
And holding tight to my
Hoard of language, hesitant to share
Golden adjectives and bejeweled verbs
But in my arched wing, I will hand
Pieces of my treasure to a trusted reader
But at the first breath of praise
I will snatch it back, place it beneath
My clawed, webbed feet and use my
Tattered wings to cover the pages of
Jewels and tarnished goblets inscribed
With language I want to keep
Close enough to my heart
To stay safe
As long
As I am.

everything seems simple until you think about it
    — Audrey Niffenegger, The Time Traveler's Wife

You ask,
Again,
May I kiss you?
I assent, nod,
Squeeze your hand,
Tightly,
Letting you know that,
For the moment,
"I am okay"
And I will let you love me
As long as my body allows
Because while I trust you,
The reflexes have a different memory
Of a different body
That didn't stop to ask for directions
And I have to take it slow,
Rocking your name between my
Tongue and cheek,
Oliver, Oliver, Oliver,
Safe, Safe, Safe
To remind myself
That I deserve to be loved
In body and soul
And while I am whole
With or without you,
I trust your guided touch
And I am in good hands
Who stop to hold me
As soon as my mind
Thinks it's all too much
And I know that love
Is not a biproduct of my body

Or a shackle on my wrist
But a candle I burn
To stay warm and bright
And I am a bird
With wings wide enough
To soar alone
But I will walk with you
As the light fades to rain that
Washes the sins we never forgave
Away into the gutter
On an unmarked street
And I lay beside you,
Rocked to sleep
By your gentle heartbeat.

the intertextuality of intercourse

Two days later
I'm picking up the clothes
You peeled from my skin
Before we had sex
For the very first time.
It's another first, cleaning up
Not from messes you've made,
But from choices you wouldn't
Undo even if they could be undone.

My eraser I used to fix
The imperfections on a drawing I
Sketched yesterday somehow
Ended up in the bra on the floor
As I put the sketch pad down,
Collapsing into a sleep that
Did not begin with whispers
Of inferiority.

I haven't fallen
Asleep without them in a while.

It's foolish to believe that something
As simple as your body in mine
Could fix me.

But perhaps it is not sex,
But the idea that I could trust enough
To let you in that means
I might be growing well.

love is fiction we choose to believe

He asked to see me today.

I told him I needed some space
And he told me he loved me either way.

I sit in Anna Rose
Working on my latest
Over ambitious project(s),
Some poetry, a screenplay,
Bits and pieces of a novel
I'll stitch together some day.

I can't help but wonder
What Oliver would think
Of each piece. I smile to
Myself, knowing full well he is, by far,
The worst editor I've ever met.
He holds each piece as though
They are a priceless manuscript
And when pressed to offer feedback,
He offers only more praise.

He fails to see why I want to improve
Because he already thinks I am perfect.

minutiae

I never noticed
The soft hair that
Grows on the back of your hand
And on the knuckles of your fingers.
I am so used to holding them
But sometimes forget to stop
And stare.

i refuse to believe in fate, but your eyes make me come close

I've never been a sucker for sonnets,
But you, you and your drowsy hair make
My fingers dance and willingly bare its
Weight, the world, if it means they get to take
Hold of you, to peruse your skin, set their
Sights on communing with you, a pair of
Feet tapping to the beat of the earth. Care
To tell me why you, the universe, stuff
Of dreams collaborated to make love
Warm, safe, something that looks like a design
That no one but God could create. Above
Our bodies, muses sing, give me a sign,
You, the eighth wonder of the world sat on
A hillside I save for myself to roam.

complicated and worth keeping

He brings roses, Merlot,
And his copy of Memento
That he had to riffle through
His parents' basement to find.
He gently blows the dust
From the cover and I
Navigate him through the
Eighteen steps necessary
To operate the DVD player.
I joke, tell him
"Just pick something on Netflix
Next time" and he tells me to
Hush, otherwise
He'll bring a VHS next time.
The film starts, ends as
It begins and we watch
Leonard retrace his steps
And nothing makes sense
But Oliver asks if he may
Hold my hand and I ask
If I may kiss his cheek
And for the moment things
Are simple, content for now
Without the answers we seek.

am i allowed to say i love you yet?

He set the table tonight.
Sure, I picked up the growing cold
Lo mein, but when I arrived,
The table was set, ready for
Me – us –
And all I needed was to sit,
And he grabbed
Serving spoons
And our own bottle of Kikkoman's
And there was no candlelight
But his eyes,
Bright enough to make me feel
As though the reiteration
Of my mundane Monday
Was nothing short
Of Shakespeare.

the earth stopped asking permission to move

Lukewarm tea, stale powdered crust, burnt scones from a box.
Debilitate. D-E-B-I-L-I-T, add to *ate,* I left unwisely by the triple point.
My grandmother's rosy cheeks bookend a sheepish smile.
I have to score the word. Math no longer comes easy to her.

Scrabble, rain, and coffee, the trinity
Of afternoons wasted on the young
And those for whom time passes differently.

It's a miracle she's still around.
The rheumatoid rears its ugly mug.

Satiate. S-A-T-I-A-T-E. I pluralize
Her pain, *Debilitates,* now an action rather
Than an optional command,
And the scores are tied.

panic attacks packaged in film

His roommates don't understand why I
Left the room so quickly when their villain
Grabbed her hijab with the same fist that pried
My hair from nape of neck, still now my skin
Prickles sore with thoughts of him, the silver
Screen between this man and me, his stale grin
Is all too close because if he takes her
Then I will find his fingers stuck in my
Hair and his tongue in my throat, his taut burn
In my constricted chest, weighing my cry
And whispered breath. I lock my windows, close
Fast the door, but his lips still slowly sigh
Inadequacies in my sleep, lose whatever repose
I pretended I could keep.

i wish curing myself for myself was enough

Believe me. For you, I would
Command the rain to rise
To unsuspecting Heavens
So that you might feel the sun again.

But commanding my body rise
From its sullen form on
Your grandmother's antique carpet
Is more than I can bare,
Because there's something there
In the grit and grime that seeps daily from
Our shoes, I lie and wait for a time
When a knife doesn't look
Like a kiss and I wait for vines
To grow from this forever borrowed carpet in your apartment
To pin me to the ground,
To keep me safe and sound,
Because the kitchen is a mausoleum
Begging to borrow my thorned crown.

three's a company

He came to
Therapy with me
Today. He held
My knee when
I cried, he
Let me speak
And he spoke
When I asked
Him to. He
Drove me home.
He held me.
I'm proud of
You. Life is
Ugly, messy, and
Cruel. But you're
Worth sharing my
Mess with and
I can finally
Admit to myself
That "I'm in
Love with you."

i deserve a fuller character arc

Irreplaceable you,
A thought my tongue
Cannot articulate,
A song my voice
Has no capacity to encompass,
My fingers ensnare themselves in
Your hair and trace miles
Of love letters on your shoulder,
Stomach, back, thigh as we
Lay inexplicably tangled
At the foot of some movie
We each conceded to because we
Each thought the other
Wanted to watch it.
Something predictable
Happens before the credits roll
And we laugh because *of course*
He got the girl and my laughter thins
Later that night as we fall asleep
On the floor because
My eyes light up the same way
The stock female lead's do
When the only round character strides in the room
And I wonder if I must barter
My developed plotline
In order to be in love.

millennial pipedream

They can keep their white picket fence,
I don't need a mailbox with our name,
Give me a mail slot and an inexpensive
Apartment key, fun sized paradise, frame
Candid photographs, arrange plants and
Plastic butterflies to match my stomach as it caves
Under your careful eyes, imagine, if you can,
Some reject, pound pup waiting to jump, too much
Spunk, head over heels to occupy your lap, you understand
How we both want, desperately, to be your love. Touch
My thigh, wind your fingers around
Kant, Christe, O'Connor, books that brush
Our fingers as we hold each other on Sunday, nestled on the ground.

compromise

"I want a canopy bed"
I utter one Sunday afternoon, my finger
Lazily swirling the spoon of a teacup,
Reading some fatalistic article in the paper
About how millennials are killing one industry or another.

You mean like a four-poster bed? you return
Skeptically, your toast
Half peanut buttered.

"I guess." I roll *four-poster* over with my tongue.
It sounds too rigid.
Can I ask why?
I shrug, the thought seeming silly
When it's loaded under my tongue.
"I don't know. It would feel like having a sleepover
In a tent every night."
You put your hand on my coffee stirring fingers.
Not yet, baby.

I shrug.

But I can make one hell of a fort out of pillows
And your devious smile pulls me into the living room
Where halfway through the fort,
Our drywall becomes ammunition
In a pillow fight that tears us across the apartment
Until you concede to my superior forces in the kitchen
And we draw truces on each other's backs
In the poster-less bedroom.

i love you always. time is nothing
— Audrey Niffenegger, The Time Traveler's Wife

You're a guarded reader.
Your eyes follow the page
Like counting birds on a telephone line
And I've never seen
Anyone
Read as slowly as you do.
You consider each character in kind,
Each question-mark or blue-jay
Worthy of retrospect in your eyes,
I suppose. All I know as I
Watch you read is your eyebrows
Furrow against their will occasionally
Betraying
Suspicion? Amusement? Empathy?
I ask if you enjoy the book and
You tell me
Yes
But give little reason why.
You are a careful thinker,
Thorough, constant, and perhaps
A bit unsure although
I constantly assure you that
What you need to believe
Is true,
Always.

i am

I want the light in my eyes
To be contagious, want the
Sinew in my thighs to evoke
Another's self-forgiveness.
I want my toes to teach
Her that it was never a sin
To dance. I want my neck to
Be held high enough to be a beacon,
I want my ears to believe that
Listening is life changing. I want
My heart to be an organ
That belongs to itself, not donated
At another's discretion. I want
My fire to burn roses because
I am a gift unto myself.

A time to grow

Sarah Henry
is the owner
of Still Poetry
Photography and
loves using writing,
photography,
and film as
means to explore
the expression
of her small
understanding of
her corner of the
universe.

For more of her work, find her at
www.stillpoetryphotography.com
&
www.isimplywrite.com

Cover art and sketches by Caitlyn Fong